CROCK·POT®
◆ THE ORIGINAL SLOW COOKER ◆

CLASSIC RECIPES

Publications International, Ltd.

Photography: Stephen Hamilton Photographics, Inc.
Photographers: Tate Hunt, Raymond Barrera
Photographers' Assistants: Chris Gurley, Allison Lazard
Prop Stylist: Tom Hamilton
Food Stylists: Kim Hartman, Rick Longhi
Assistant Food Stylist: Breana Moeller

Pictured on the front cover: Grandma Ruth's Minestrone *(page 96)*.

ISBN-13: 978-1-4127-2834-8
ISBN-10: 1-4127-2834-7

Library of Congress Control Number:

Manufactured in China.

8 7 6 5 4 3 2 1

Contents

Slow-Cooking
HINTS AND TIPS

Slow Cooker Sizes

Smaller slow cookers, such as 1- to 3½-quart models, are the perfect size for singles, a couple, empty-nesters and for serving dips.

While medium-size slow cookers (those holding somewhere between 3 and 5 quarts) will easily cook enough food to feed a small family, they're also convenient for holiday side dishes and appetizers.

Large slow cookers are great for big family dinners, holiday entertaining, and potluck suppers. A 6- to 7-quart model is ideal if you like to make meals in advance and have dinner tonight and store leftovers for another day.

Types of Slow Cookers

Current models of **Crock-Pot®** slow cookers come equipped with many different features and benefits, from auto-cook programs, to stovetop-safe stoneware, to timed programming. Visit www.crockpot.com to find the slow cooker that best suits your needs and lifestyle.

Cooking, Stirring, and Food Safety

Crock-Pot® slow cookers are safe to leave unattended. The outer heating base may get hot as it cooks, but it should not pose a fire hazard. The heating element in the heating base functions at a low wattage and is safe for your countertops.

Your slow cooker should be filled at least one-half to three-quarters full for most recipes unless otherwise instructed. Lean meats, such as chicken or pork tenderloin, will cook faster than meats with more connective tissue and fat, such as beef chuck or pork shoulder. Bone-in meats will take longer than boneless cuts. Typical slow cooker dishes take 7 to 8 hours to reach the simmer point on LOW and 3 to 4 hours on HIGH. Once the vegetables and meat begin to simmer and braise, their flavors will fully blend and the meat will become fall-off-the bone tender.

According to the United States Department of Agriculture, all bacteria are killed at a temperature of 165°F. It's important to follow the recommended cooking times and to avoid opening the lid often, especially early in the cooking process when heat is building up inside the unit. If you need to open the lid to check on your food or are adding additional ingredients, remember to allow additional cooking time, if necessary, to ensure food is thoroughly cooked and tender.

Large slow cookers, the 6- to 7-quart sizes, may benefit from a quick stir halfway through the cook time to help distribute heat and promote even cooking. It is usually unnecessary to stir at all since even ½ cup of liquid will help to distribute heat, and the crockery is the perfect medium for holding food at an even temperature throughout the cooking process.

Oven-Safe

All **Crock-Pot®** slow cooker removable crockery inserts may (without their lids) be used in ovens at up to 400°F safely. Also, all **Crock-Pot®** slow cookers are microwavable without their lids. If you own another brand slow cooker, please refer to your owner's manual for advice on oven and microwave safety.

Frozen Food

Frozen or partially frozen food can be cooked in a slow cooker; however, it will require a longer cooking time than the same recipe made with fresh food. Using an instant-read thermometer is recommended to ensure meat is completely cooked.

Pasta and Rice

If you're converting a recipe that calls for uncooked pasta, cook the pasta according to the package directions just until tender before adding it to the slow cooker. If you are converting a recipe that calls for cooked rice, stir in the raw rice with other ingredients; add ¼ cup of extra liquid per ¼ cup of raw rice.

Beans

Beans must be softened completely before they're combined with sugar and/or acidic foods. Sugar and acid have a hardening effect on beans and will prevent softening. Fully cooked canned beans may be used as a substitute for dried beans.

Vegetables

Root vegetables often cook more slowly than meat. Cut vegetables into small pieces so that they cook at the same rate as the meat, large or small, lean or marbled. Place them near the sides or on the bottom of the stoneware so that they will cook more quickly.

Herbs

Fresh herbs add flavor and color when they're added at the end of the cooking time, but for dishes with shorter cook times, hearty fresh herbs such as rosemary and thyme hold up well. If added at the beginning, the flavor of many fresh herbs lessen over long cook times. Ground and/or dried herbs and spices work well in slow cooking because they retain their flavor, and may be added at beginning. The flavor power of all herbs and spices can vary greatly depending on their particular strength and shelf life. Use chili powders and garlic powder sparingly because they often intensify over long cook times. Always taste the finished dish adjust the seasonings, including salt and pepper, before serving.

Liquids

It's not necessary to use more than ½ to 1 cup of liquid in most instances since the juices in meats and vegetables are retained in slow cooking more so than in conventional cooking. Excess liquid can be reduced and concentrated after slow cooking either on the stovetop or by removing meat and vegetables from stoneware, stirring in cornstarch or tapioca, and setting the slow cooker to HIGH. Cook on HIGH for approximately 15 minutes or until the juices are thickened.

Milk

Milk, cream, and sour cream break down during extended cooking. When possible, add them during the last 15 to 30 minutes of cooking, until just heated through. Condensed soups may be substituted for milk and can cook for extended times.

Fish

Fish is delicate and it should be stirred in gently during the last 15 to 30 minutes of cooking time. Cook just until cooked through, and serve immediately.

Classic Appetizers

Curried Snack Mix

- 3 tablespoons butter
- 2 tablespoons packed light brown sugar
- 1½ teaspoons hot curry powder
- ¼ teaspoon salt
- ¼ teaspoon ground cumin
- 2 cups rice cereal squares
- 1 cup walnut halves
- 1 cup dried cranberries

Melt butter in large skillet. Add brown sugar, curry powder, salt and cumin; mix well. Add cereal, walnuts and cranberries; stir to coat. Transfer mixture to 4½-quart **CROCK-POT®** slow cooker. Cover; cook on LOW 3 hours. Remove cover; cook, uncovered, 30 minutes.

| Makes 16 servings | Prep Time: 5 minutes | Cook Time: 3½ hours (LOW) |

Easy Taco Dip

½ **pound ground beef chuck**
1 **cup frozen corn**
½ **cup chopped onion**
½ **cup salsa**
½ **cup mild taco sauce**
1 **can (4 ounces) diced mild green chiles**
1 **can (4 ounces) sliced black olives, drained**
1 **cup (4 ounces) shredded Mexican cheese blend**
Tortilla chips
Sour cream

1. Brown ground beef in large nonstick skillet over medium-high heat, stirring to break up meat. Drain fat. Spoon into 4½-quart **CROCK-POT®** slow cooker.

2. Add corn, onion, salsa, taco sauce, chiles and olives to **CROCK-POT®** slow cooker; mix well. Cover; cook on LOW 2 to 3 hours.

3. Just before serving, stir in cheese. Serve with tortilla chips and sour cream.

Tip: To keep this dip hot through an entire party, simply leave it in the **CROCK-POT®** slow cooker on LOW.

Makes about 3 cups dip   *Prep Time:* 15 minutes   *Cook Time:* 2 to 3 hours (LOW)

Honey-Mustard Chicken Wings

3 pounds chicken wings
1 teaspoon salt
1 teaspoon black pepper
½ cup honey
½ cup barbecue sauce
2 tablespoons spicy brown mustard
1 clove garlic, minced
3 to 4 thin lemon slices

1. Cut off chicken wing tips; discard. Cut each wing at joint to make 2 pieces. Sprinkle with salt and pepper; place wing pieces on broiler rack. Broil 4 to 5 inches from heat about 10 minutes, turning halfway through cooking time. Place in 4½-quart **CROCK-POT®** slow cooker.

2. Combine honey, barbecue sauce, mustard and garlic in small bowl; mix well. Pour sauce over chicken wings. Top with lemon slices. Cover; cook on LOW 4 to 5 hours.

3. Remove and discard lemon slices. Serve wings with sauce.

Makes about 24 wings   *Prep Time:* 20 minutes   *Cook Time:* 4 to 5 hours (LOW)

Creamy Artichoke-Parmesan Dip

- 2 cans (14 ounces each) artichoke hearts, drained and chopped
- 2 cups (8 ounces) shredded mozzarella cheese
- 1½ cups grated Parmesan cheese
- 1½ cups mayonnaise
- ½ cup finely chopped onion
- ½ teaspoon dried oregano
- ¼ teaspoon garlic powder
- 4 loaves pita bread
  Assorted cut-up vegetables

1. Combine all ingredients except pita bread and cut-up vegetables in 1½-quart **CROCK-POT®** slow cooker; mix well.

2. Cover; cook on LOW 2 hours.

3. Just before serving, cut pita into wedges. Arrange pita and vegetables on platter; serve with warm dip.

Makes 4 cups dip   *Prep Time:* 10 minutes   *Cook Time:* 2 hours (LOW)

Chili con Queso

1 package (16 ounces) pasteurized processed cheese spread, cubed
1 can (10 ounces) diced tomatoes with green chiles
1 cup sliced green onions
2 teaspoons ground coriander
2 teaspoons ground cumin
¾ teaspoon hot pepper sauce
Green onion strips (optional)
Hot pepper slices (optional)
Tortilla chips

1. Combine cheese spread, tomatoes, green onions, coriander and cumin in 1½-quart **CROCK-POT®** slow cooker; stir until well blended.

2. Cover; cook on LOW 2 to 3 hours or until hot.*

3. Garnish with green onion strips and hot pepper slices, if desired. Serve with tortilla chips.

Serving Suggestion: Serve Chili con Queso with tortilla chips. For something different, cut pita bread into triangles and toast them in a preheated 400°F oven for 5 minutes or until they are crisp.

Dip will be very hot; use caution when serving.

| Makes 3 cups | Prep Time: 10 minutes | Cook Time: 2 to 3 hours (LOW) |

Chablis-Infused Swiss Fondue

3 cups Chablis or other white wine
2 teaspoons lemon juice
½ teaspoon grated lemon peel
1½ pounds Swiss cheese, shredded
3 tablespoons all-purpose flour
3 tablespoons kirsch or cherry brandy
1 teaspoon mace, freshly ground
1 teaspoon black pepper
½ teaspoon paprika
1 loaf crusty Italian peasant bread, cut into 1½-inch cubes
Fresh vegetables, cut up for dipping

1. Place wine, lemon juice and lemon peel in saucepan over medium-high heat. Bring to a simmer.

2. Combine cheese and flour in medium mixing bowl. Gradually add cheese to saucepan, stirring constantly, until cheese is completely melted. Add kirsch and stir well to combine. Add mace, pepper and paprika, and stir again thoroughly.

3. Pour cheese mixture into 5- to 6-quart **CROCK-POT®** slow cooker. Cover; cook on HIGH 30 minutes. Reduce heat to LOW, and cook 2 to 5 hours longer, stirring occasionally. Serve with Italian bread and vegetables.

Makes 6 to 8 servings	*Prep Time:* 15 minutes	*Cook Time:* 30 minutes (HIGH) plus 2 to 5 hours (LOW)

Caponata

    1 medium eggplant (about 1 pound), peeled and cut into
        ½-inch pieces
    1 can (about 14 ounces) diced Italian plum tomatoes
    1 medium onion, chopped
    1 red bell pepper, cut into ½-inch pieces
    ½ cup medium-hot salsa
    ¼ cup extra-virgin olive oil
    2 tablespoons capers, drained
    2 tablespoons balsamic vinegar
    3 cloves garlic, minced
    1 teaspoon dried oregano
    ¼ teaspoon salt
    ⅓ cup packed fresh basil, cut into thin strips
        Toasted sliced Italian or French bread

1. Combine eggplant, tomatoes, onion, bell pepper, salsa, oil, capers, vinegar, garlic, oregano and salt in 4½-quart **CROCK-POT®** slow cooker. Cover; cook on LOW 7 to 8 hours or until vegetables are crisp-tender.

2. Stir in basil. Serve at room temperature on toasted bread.

| Makes about 5¼ cups | *Prep Time:* 15 minutes | *Cook Time:* 7 to 8 hours (LOW) |

Best Asian-Style Ribs

2 **full racks baby back pork ribs, split into 3 sections each**
6 **ounces hoisin sauce**
2 **tablespoons minced fresh ginger**
½ **cup maraschino cherries**
½ **cup rice wine vinegar**
  Water to cover
4 **green onions, chopped**

Combine ribs, hoisin sauce, ginger, cherries, vinegar and water in 4½-quart **CROCK-POT®** slow cooker. Cover; cook on LOW 6 to 7 hours or on HIGH 3 to 3½ hours or until pork is done. Sprinkle with green onions before serving.

Makes 6 to 8 servings   *Prep Time:* 10 to 15 minutes   *Cook Time:* 6 to 7 hours (LOW) or 3 to 3½ hours (HIGH)

Spicy Sweet & Sour Cocktail Franks

2 packages (8 ounces each) cocktail franks
½ cup ketchup or chili sauce
½ cup apricot preserves
1 teaspoon hot pepper sauce
Additional hot pepper sauce (optional)

1. Combine all ingredients in 1½-quart **CROCK-POT®** slow cooker; mix well. Cover; cook on LOW 2 to 3 hours.

2. Serve warm or at room temperature with additional hot pepper sauce, if desired.

Makes about 4 dozen cocktail franks   *Prep Time:* 8 minutes   *Cook Time:* 2 to 3 hours (LOW)

Party Mix

3 cups bite-size rice cereal squares
2 cups toasted oat ring cereal
2 cups bite-size wheat cereal squares
1 cup peanuts or pistachio nuts
1 cup thin pretzel sticks
½ cup (1 stick) butter, melted
1 tablespoon Worcestershire sauce
1 teaspoon seasoned salt
½ teaspoon garlic powder
⅛ teaspoon ground red pepper (optional)

1. Combine cereals, nuts and pretzels in 4½-quart **CROCK-POT®** slow cooker.

2. Mix butter, Worcestershire sauce, seasoned salt, garlic powder and red pepper, if desired, in small bowl. Pour over cereal mixture in **CROCK-POT®** slow cooker; toss lightly to coat.

3. Cover; cook on LOW 3 hours, stirring well every 30 minutes. Cook, uncovered, 30 minutes more. Store cooled Party Mix in airtight container.

Makes 10 cups   **Prep Time:** 15 minutes   **Cook Time:** 3½ hours (LOW)

Maple-Glazed Meatballs

1½ **cups ketchup**

1 **cup maple syrup or maple-flavored syrup**

⅓ **cup reduced-sodium soy sauce**

1 **tablespoon quick-cooking tapioca**

1½ **teaspoons ground allspice**

1 **teaspoon dry mustard**

2 **packages (about 16 ounces each) frozen fully cooked meatballs, partially thawed and separated**

1 **can (20 ounces) pineapple chunks in juice, drained**

1. Combine ketchup, maple syrup, soy sauce, tapioca, allspice and mustard in 4½-quart **CROCK-POT®** slow cooker.

2. Carefully stir meatballs and pineapple chunks into ketchup mixture.

3. Cover; cook on LOW 5 to 6 hours. Stir before serving.

Variation: Serve over hot cooked rice for an entrée.

Makes about 48 meatballs　　　*Prep Time:* 10 minutes　　　*Cook Time:* 5 to 6 hours (LOW)

Pizza Fondue

½ **pound bulk Italian sausage**
1 **cup chopped onion**
2 **jars (26 ounces each) meatless pasta sauce**
4 **ounces thinly sliced ham, finely chopped**
1 **package (3 ounces) sliced pepperoni, finely chopped**
¼ **teaspoon red pepper flakes**
1 **pound mozzarella cheese, cut into ¾-inch cubes**
1 **loaf Italian or French bread, cut into 1-inch cubes**

1. Brown sausage and onion in large skillet over medium-high heat until sausage is no longer pink, stirring to break up meat. Drain fat. Transfer sausage mixture to 4½-quart **CROCK-POT®** slow cooker.

2. Stir in pasta sauce, ham, pepperoni and pepper flakes. Cover; cook on LOW 3 to 4 hours.

3. Serve fondue with cheese and bread cubes.

Makes 20 to 25 servings   *Prep Time:* 15 minutes   *Cook Time:* 3 to 4 hours (LOW)

Brats in Beer

1½ **pounds bratwurst (about 5 or 6 links)**
1 **bottle (12 ounces) amber ale**
1 **medium onion, thinly sliced**
2 **tablespoons packed brown sugar**
2 **tablespoons red wine vinegar or cider vinegar**
  Spicy brown mustard
  Cocktail rye bread

1. Combine bratwurst, ale, onion, brown sugar and vinegar in 4½-quart **CROCK-POT®** slow cooker. Cover; cook on LOW 4 to 5 hours.

2. Remove bratwurst and onion slices from **CROCK-POT®** slow cooker. Cut bratwurst into ½-inch-thick slices. For mini open-faced sandwiches, spread mustard on cocktail rye bread. Top with bratwurst slices and cooked onion.

Tip: Choose a light-tasting beer for cooking brats.

Makes 30 to 36 appetizers   *Prep Time:* 5 minutes   *Cook Time:* 4 to 5 hours (LOW)

Sweet and Spicy Sausage Rounds

1 pound kielbasa sausage, cut into ¼-inch-thick rounds
⅔ cup blackberry jam
⅓ cup steak sauce
1 tablespoon prepared yellow mustard
½ teaspoon ground allspice

1. Place all ingredients in 4½-quart **CROCK-POT®** slow cooker; toss to coat completely. Cook on HIGH 3 hours or until richly glazed.

2. Serve with decorative cocktail picks.

| Makes 3 cups | *Prep Time:* 10 minutes | *Cook Time:* 3 hours (HIGH) |

Favorite Main Dishes

Pork Roast with Fruit Medley

- 1 **cup water**
- ½ **cup kosher or coarse salt**
- 2 **tablespoons sugar**
- 1 **teaspoon dried thyme**
- 2 **whole bay leaves**
- 1 **pork roast (about 4 pounds)**
- 3 **tablespoons olive oil**
- 2 **cups green grapes**
- 1 **cup dried apricots**
- 1 **cup dried prunes**
- 2 **cloves garlic, minced**
- 1 **cup red wine**
  Juice of ½ lemon

1. Combine water, salt, sugar, thyme and bay leaves in large resealable food storage bag or in plastic or glass container (do not use metal container). Add pork roast. Marinate overnight or up to 2 days in refrigerator, turning occasionally.

2. Remove roast from brine and lightly pat dry. Heat oil in skillet over medium heat until hot. Brown pork roast on all sides, cooking 5 to 10 minutes, turning as it browns. Transfer to 4½-quart **CROCK-POT®** slow cooker.

3. Add remaining ingredients. Stir gently to combine. Cover; cook on LOW 7 to 9 hours or on HIGH 3 to 5 hours. Serve over rice or couscous.

Makes 6 to 8 servings	*Prep Time:* 15 minutes, plus marinating	*Cook Time:* 7 to 9 hours (LOW) or 3 to 5 hours (HIGH)

Favorite Main Dishes 35

Beef Bourguignon

6 strips bacon, cut into 1- to 2-inch pieces
3 pounds beef rump roast, cut into 1-inch cubes
1 large carrot, peeled and sliced
1 medium onion, sliced
1 teaspoon salt
½ teaspoon black pepper
3 tablespoons all-purpose flour
1 can (10 ounces) condensed beef broth
2 cups red wine (such as Burgundy)
1 pound fresh mushrooms, sliced
½ pound small white onions, peeled
1 tablespoon tomato paste
2 cloves garlic, minced
½ teaspoon dried thyme
1 whole bay leaf

1. Cook bacon in skillet over medium heat until crisp. Remove; set aside.

2. Add beef to skillet and brown well. Remove; set aside.

3. Brown carrot and onion in skillet. Transfer to 4½-quart **CROCK-POT®** slow cooker. Season with salt and pepper. Stir in flour, add broth and mix well. Stir in beef and bacon.

4. Add wine, mushrooms, onions, tomato paste, garlic, thyme and bay leaf. Cover; cook on LOW 10 to 12 hours or HIGH 5 to 6 hours.

Makes 6 to 8 servings	Prep Time: 15 minutes	Cook Time: 10 to 12 hours (LOW) or 5 to 6 hours (HIGH)

Polenta with Beef Chile Sauce

    2 tablespoons vegetable oil
    2 pounds beef round roast, cut into bite-size pieces
    1 yellow onion, peeled and finely chopped
    2 cloves garlic, diced
 1¾ cups water
    5 canned whole green chiles, peeled and diced
    1 chipotle chile, diced
    1 teaspoon salt
    1 teaspoon all-purpose flour
    1 teaspoon dried oregano
  ½ teaspoon ground cumin
  ¼ teaspoon black pepper
    1 package (16 ounces) prepared polenta
      Fresh cilantro (optional)

1. Heat oil in large skillet over medium heat until hot. Sear beef on all sides, turning as it browns. Add onions and garlic during last few minutes of searing. Transfer to 4½-quart **CROCK-POT®** slow cooker.

2. Add water and chiles. Stir well to combine. Cover; cook on LOW 2 hours.

3. Combine salt, flour, oregano, cumin and black pepper in small bowl. Add to **CROCK-POT®** slow cooker. Stir well to combine. Cover; cook on LOW 3 to 4 hours longer.

4. Turn **CROCK-POT®** slow cooker to warm. Slice polenta into ½-inch-thick rounds. Place on greased baking sheet. Broil until crispy, about 4 minutes on each side. To serve, place polenta rounds on individual plates and spoon meat and sauce over polenta. Garnish with fresh cilantro, if desired.

Makes 4 to 6 servings   *Prep Time:* 15 minutes   *Cook Time:* 5 to 6 hours (LOW)

Fiery Southwestern Enchiladas

Steak Filling

2 pounds tri-tip steak, cut into large chunks
1 cup water
½ cup tequila
5 cloves garlic, minced
1 serrano pepper,* diced
1 jalapeño pepper,* diced
Kosher salt and freshly ground black pepper, to taste

Enchilada Sauce

5 cans (7 ounces each) tomatillo sauce
1½ cups tomato sauce
1 pound Monterey Jack cheese, grated, divided
3 cans (15½ ounces each) black beans, rinsed and drained
1 can (8 ounces) corn, drained
16 flour tortillas
1 can (7 ounces) diced mild green chiles
½ cup sour cream (optional)
1 cup chopped fresh tomato
¼ cup chives, chopped

*Serrano and jalapeño peppers can sting and irritate the skin; wear rubber gloves when handling peppers and do not touch eyes. Wash hands after handling.

1. One day ahead, make the steak. Combine steak, water, tequila, garlic and peppers in 4½-quart **CROCK-POT®** slow cooker. Season with salt and pepper. Cover; cook on LOW 10 to 12 hours or until very tender. Shred steak. Refrigerate until ready to use.

2. For the enchilada sauce, combine tomatillo and tomato sauces in saucepan over medium heat. Cook, stirring, until hot. Stir in ¼ cup cheese.

3. Heat beans and corn in another saucepan. Fill tortillas with sauce, beans, corn, cheese, steak and diced chiles, leaving enough cheese, sauce and diced chilies for topping. Roll each tortilla. Arrange rolls in greased baking pan. Pour remaining sauce over the top. Sprinkle with remaining cheese and diced chiles.

4. Cover pan with foil and bake 15 minutes. Top with sour cream, if desired, tomato and chives. Serve immediately.

Makes 8 servings   *Prep Time:* 30 minutes   *Cook Time:* 10 to 12 hours (LOW)

Beef with Green Chiles

¼ **cup plus 1 tablespoon all-purpose flour, divided**
½ **teaspoon salt**
¼ **teaspoon black pepper**
1 **pound beef stew meat**
1 **tablespoon vegetable oil**
2 **cloves garlic, minced**
1 **cup beef broth**
1 **can (7 ounces) diced mild green chiles, drained**
½ **teaspoon dried oregano**
2 **tablespoons water**
  Hot cooked rice (optional)
  Diced tomato (optional)

1. Combine ¼ cup flour, salt and pepper in resealable food storage bag. Add beef; shake to coat beef. Heat oil in large skillet over medium-high heat. Add beef and garlic. Brown beef on all sides. Place beef mixture into 4½-quart **CROCK-POT®** slow cooker. Add broth to skillet scraping up any browned bits. Pour broth mixture into **CROCK-POT®** slow cooker. Add green chiles and oregano.

2. Cover; cook on LOW 7 to 8 hours. For thicker sauce, combine remaining 1 tablespoon flour and water in small bowl stirring until mixture is smooth. Stir mixture into **CROCK-POT®** slow cooker; mix well. Cover and cook until thickened.

3. Serve with rice and garnish with diced tomato, if desired.

Tip: Use 2 cans of chiles for a slightly hotter taste.

Makes 4 servings   *Prep Time:* 15 minutes   *Cook Time:* 7 to 8 hours (LOW)

Scalloped Potatoes & Ham

1 **ham steak (about 1½ pounds), cut into cubes**
6 **large russet potatoes, sliced into ¼-inch rounds**
1 **ham steak (about 1½ pounds), cut into cubes**
1 **can (10¾ ounces) condensed cream of mushroom soup**
1 **soup can water**
4 **ounces shredded Cheddar cheese**
  Grill seasoning, to taste

1. Spray inside of 4½-quart **CROCK-POT®** slow cooker with nonstick cooking spray. Layer ham and potatoes in bottom.

2. Combine soup, water, cheese and seasoning in large mixing bowl; pour over potatoes and ham.

3. Cover; cook on HIGH for about 3½ hours or until potatoes are fork tender. Turn **CROCK-POT®** slow cooker to LOW and continue cooking for 1 hour or until done.

Makes 5 to 6 servings   *Prep Time:* 15 minutes   *Cook Time:* 3½ hours (HIGH) plus 1 hour (LOW)

Stuffed Chicken Breasts

6 boneless, skinless chicken breasts
8 ounces feta cheese, crumbled
3 cups chopped fresh spinach leaves
⅓ cup oil-packed sun-dried tomatoes, drained and chopped
1 teaspoon minced lemon peel
1 teaspoon dried basil, oregano or mint
½ teaspoon garlic powder
Freshly ground black pepper, to taste
1 can (15 ounces) diced tomatoes, undrained
½ cup oil-cured olives*
Hot cooked polenta

*If using pitted olives, add to CROCK-POT® slow cooker in the final hour of cooking.

1. Place chicken breast between 2 pieces of plastic wrap. Using meat mallet or back of skillet, pound breast until about ¼ inch thick. Repeat with remaining chicken.

2. Combine feta, spinach, sun-dried tomatoes, lemon peel, basil, garlic powder and pepper in medium bowl.

3. Lay pounded chicken, smooth side down, on work surface. Place about 2 tablespoons feta mixture on wide end of breast. Roll tightly. Repeat with remaining chicken.

4. Place rolled chicken, seam side down, in 4½-quart **CROCK-POT®** slow cooker. Top with diced tomatoes with juice and olives. Cover; cook on LOW 5½ to 6 hours or on HIGH 4 hours. Serve with polenta.

Makes 6 servings   *Prep Time:* 20 minutes   *Cook Time:* 5½ to 6 hours (LOW) or 4 hours (HIGH)

Shrimp Creole

¼ cup (½ stick) butter
1 onion, chopped
¼ cup biscuit baking mix
3 cups water
1 cup chopped celery
1 cup chopped green bell pepper
2 cans (6 ounces each) tomato paste
2 teaspoons salt
½ teaspoon sugar
2 bay leaves
   Black pepper, to taste
4 pounds shrimp, peeled, deveined and cleaned
   Hot cooked rice

1. Cook and stir butter and onion in medium skillet until onion is tender. Stir in biscuit mix. Place mixture in 4½-quart **CROCK-POT®** slow cooker.

2. Add water, celery, bell pepper, tomato paste, salt, sugar, bay leaves and black pepper. Cover; cook on LOW 6 to 8 hours.

3. Turn **CROCK-POT®** slow cooker to HIGH and add shrimp. Cook 45 minutes to 1 hour or until shrimp are done. Remove bay leaves. Serve over rice.

Makes 8 to 10 servings   *Prep Time:* 25 minutes   *Cook Time:* 6 to 8 hours (LOW) plus 45 minutes to 1 hour (HIGH)

Chipotle Chicken Casserole

1 pound boneless, skinless chicken thighs, cut into cubes
1 teaspoon salt
1 teaspoon ground cumin
1 bay leaf
1 chipotle pepper in adobo sauce, minced
1 medium onion, diced
1 can (15 ounces) navy beans, rinsed and drained
1 can (15 ounces) black beans, rinsed and drained
1 can (14½ ounces) crushed tomatoes, undrained
1½ cups chicken broth
½ cup orange juice
¼ cup chopped fresh cilantro (optional)

Combine chicken, salt, cumin, bay leaf, chipotle pepper, onion, beans, tomatoes with juice, broth and orange juice in 4½-quart **CROCK-POT®** slow cooker. Cover; cook on LOW 7 to 8 hours or on HIGH 3½ to 4 hours. Remove bay leaf before serving. Garnish with cilantro, if desired.

Makes 6 servings	*Prep Time:* 10 to 15 minutes	*Cook Time:* 7 to 8 hours (LOW) or 3½ to 4 hours (HIGH)

Turkey with Chunky Cherry Relish

1 bag (16 ounces) frozen dark cherries, coarsely chopped
1 can (about 14 ounces) diced tomatoes with jalapeños
1 package (6 ounces) dried cherry-flavored cranberries or dried cherries, coarsely chopped
2 small onions, thinly sliced
1 small green bell pepper, chopped
½ cup packed brown sugar
2 tablespoons tapioca
1½ tablespoons salt
½ teaspoon ground cinnamon
½ teaspoon black pepper
1 bone-in turkey breast (about 2½ to 3 pounds)
2 tablespoons water
1 tablespoon cornstarch

1. Place cherries, tomatoes, cranberries, onions, bell pepper, brown sugar, tapioca, salt, cinnamon and black pepper in 4½-quart **CROCK-POT®** slow cooker; mix well.

2. Place turkey on top of mixture. Cover; cook on LOW 7 to 8 hours or until temperature registers over 170°F on meat thermometer inserted into thickest part of breast, not touching bone. Remove turkey from **CROCK-POT®** slow cooker; keep warm.

3. Increase temperature to HIGH. Combine water and cornstarch in small bowl to form smooth paste. Stir into cherry mixture. Cook, uncovered, on HIGH 15 minutes or until sauce is thickened. Adjust seasonings, if desired. Slice turkey and top with relish.

Makes 4 to 6 servings	*Prep Time:* 20 minutes	*Cook Time:* 7 to 8 hours (LOW) plus 15 minutes (HIGH)

Roast Chicken with Peas, Prosciutto and Cream

  1 whole roasting chicken (about 2½ pounds), cut up
    Salt and black pepper, to taste
  5 ounces prosciutto, diced
  1 small white onion, finely chopped
  ½ cup dry white wine
  1 package (10 ounces) frozen peas
  ½ cup heavy cream
1½ tablespoons cornstarch
  2 tablespoons water
  4 cups farfalle pasta, cooked al dente

1. Season chicken pieces with salt and pepper. Combine chicken, prosciutto, onion and wine in 4½-quart **CROCK-POT®** slow cooker. Cover; cook on LOW 8 to 10 hours or HIGH 4 to 5½ hours or until meat is fully cooked.

2. During last 30 minutes of cooking, add frozen peas and heavy cream to cooking liquid. Remove chicken when done and carve meat and set aside on a warmed platter.

3. Combine cornstarch and water. Add to cooking liquid in **CROCK-POT®** slow cooker. Cover; cook on HIGH 10 to 15 minutes or until thickened.

4. To serve, spoon pasta onto individual plates. Place chicken on pasta and top each portion with sauce.

| Makes 6 servings | *Prep Time:* 10 minutes | *Cook Time:* 8 to 10 hours (LOW) or 4 to 5½ hours (HIGH) |

Braised Beef Brisket

2 tablespoons olive oil
1 beef brisket (3 to 4 pounds)
   Salt and black pepper, to taste
5 cloves garlic, minced
1 large yellow onion, diced
2 pounds Yukon Gold potatoes, peeled and cut into ¾-inch cubes
1 pound parsnips, peeled and cut into ¼-inch slices
1 pound carrots, peeled and cut into ¼-inch slices
1 cup red wine
1 cup beef broth
¼ cup tomato paste
1 teaspoon dried thyme
1 teaspoon dried rosemary
2 whole bay leaves

1. Heat oil in skillet over medium heat until hot. Season brisket with salt and pepper. Place garlic and onions in skillet. Brown brisket with garlic and onions, about 2 to 3 minutes per side. Transfer to 4½-quart **CROCK-POT®** slow cooker.

2. Add remaining ingredients and stir well to combine. Cover; cook on LOW 5½ to 7½ hours or on HIGH 3½ to 5½ hours or until meat is cooked through and tender.

3. Remove bay leaves before slicing and serving.

Makes 6 servings	Prep Time: 15 minutes	Cook Time: 5½ to 7½ hours (LOW) or 3½ to 5½ hours (HIGH)

Boneless Pork Roast with Garlic

1 **boneless pork rib roast (2 to 2½ pounds), rinsed and patted dry**
Salt and black pepper, to taste
3 **tablespoons olive oil, divided**
4 **garlic cloves, minced**
4 **tablespoons chopped fresh rosemary**
Butcher's twine
½ **lemon, cut into ⅛- to ¼-inch slices**
¼ **cup white wine**
½ **cup chicken stock**

1. Unroll the pork roast and season with salt and black pepper. Combine 2 tablespoons oil, garlic and rosemary in small bowl. Rub over pork.

2. Roll and tie pork snugly with twine. Tuck lemon slices under twine and into ends of roast.

3. Heat remaining 1 tablespoon oil in skillet over medium heat until hot. Sear pork on all sides until just browned. Transfer to 4½-quart **CROCK-POT®** slow cooker.

4. Return skillet to heat. Add white wine and stock, stirring with wooden spoon to loosen any caramelized bits. Pour over pork. Cover; cook on LOW 8 to 9 hours or on HIGH 4 to 5 hours.

5. Transfer roast to cutting board. Allow to rest 10 minutes before removing twine and slicing. Adjust seasonings, if desired. To serve, pour pan juices over sliced pork.

| Makes 4 to 6 servings | *Prep Time:* 20 minutes | *Cook Time:* 8 to 9 hours (LOW) or 4 to 5 hours (HIGH) |

Chicken Vesuvio

3 tablespoons all-purpose flour
1½ teaspoons dried oregano
1 teaspoon salt
½ teaspoon freshly ground black pepper
1 frying chicken, cut up, or 3 pounds bone-in chicken pieces
2 tablespoons olive oil
4 small baking potatoes, scrubbed, cut into 8 wedges each
2 small onions, cut into thin wedges
4 cloves garlic, minced
¼ cup chicken broth
¼ cup dry white wine
¼ cup chopped fresh parsley
Lemon wedges (optional)

1. Combine flour, oregano, salt and pepper in a paper or large resealable food storage bag. Trim and discard excess fat from chicken. Add chicken, several pieces at a time, to bag and shake to coat lightly with flour mixture. Heat oil in large skillet over medium heat until hot. Add chicken; cook 10 to 12 minutes or until browned on all sides.

2. Place potatoes, onion and garlic in 4½-quart **CROCK-POT®** slow cooker. Add broth and wine. Top with chicken pieces; pour pan juices from skillet over chicken. Cover; cook on LOW 6 to 7 hours or on HIGH 3 to 3½ hours or until chicken and potatoes are tender.

3. Transfer chicken and vegetables to serving plates; top with juices from slow cooker. Sprinkle with parsley. Serve with lemon wedges.

Makes 4 to 6 servings   *Prep Time:* 20 minutes   *Cook Time:* 6 to 7 hours (LOW) or 3 to 3½ hours (HIGH)

Traditional Sides

Bacon and Cheese Brunch Potatoes

3 medium russet potatoes (about 2 pounds), peeled and cut into 1-inch dice
1 cup chopped onion
½ teaspoon seasoned salt
4 slices crisply cooked bacon, crumbled
1 cup (4 ounces) shredded sharp Cheddar cheese
1 tablespoon water or chicken broth

1. Coat 4½-quart **CROCK-POT®** slow cooker with cooking spray. Place half of potatoes in slow cooker. Sprinkle half of onion and seasoned salt over potatoes; top with half of bacon and cheese. Repeat layers, ending with cheese. Sprinkle water over top.

2. Cover; cook on LOW 6 hours or on HIGH 3½ hours or until potatoes and onion are tender. Stir gently to mix and serve hot.

Makes 6 servings   *Prep Time:* 10 minutes   *Cook Time:* 6 hours (LOW) or 3½ hours (HIGH)

Old-Fashioned Sauerkraut

      8 **slices bacon, chopped**
      2 **pounds sauerkraut**
      1 **large head cabbage or 2 small heads**
  2½ **cups chopped onions**
      4 **tablespoons (½ stick) butter**
      2 **tablespoons sugar**
      1 **teaspoon salt**
      1 **teaspoon black pepper**

1. Heat skillet over medium heat until hot. Cook and stir bacon until crisp. Remove skillet from heat and set aside. (Do not drain bacon fat.)

2. Place sauerkraut, cabbage, onions, butter, sugar, salt and pepper in 4½-quart **CROCK-POT®** slow cooker. Pour bacon and bacon fat over sauerkraut mixture. Cover; cook on LOW 4 to 5 hours or on HIGH 1 to 3 hours.

Note: Add your favorite bratwurst, knockwurst or other sausage to this recipe to make an entire meal.

Makes 8 to 10 servings	*Prep Time:* 15 to 20 minutes	*Cook Time:* 4 to 5 hours (LOW) or 1 to 3 hours (HIGH)

Creamy Curried Spinach

3 packages (10 ounces each) frozen spinach, thawed
1 onion, chopped
4 teaspoons minced garlic
2 tablespoons curry powder
2 tablespoons butter, melted
¼ cup chicken broth
¼ cup heavy cream
1 teaspoon lemon juice

Combine spinach, onion, garlic, curry powder, butter and broth in 4½-quart **CROCK-POT®** slow cooker. Cover; cook on LOW 3 to 4 hours or on HIGH 2 hours or until done. Stir in cream and lemon juice 30 minutes before end of cooking time.

Makes 6 to 8 servings   *Prep Time:* 10 to 15 minutes   *Cook Time:* 3 to 4 hours (LOW) or 2 hours (HIGH)

Easy Dirty Rice

½ **pound bulk Italian sausage**
2 **cups water**
1 **cup uncooked long grain rice**
1 **large onion, finely chopped**
1 **large green bell pepper, finely chopped**
½ **cup finely chopped celery**
1½ **teaspoons salt**
½ **teaspoon ground red pepper**
½ **cup chopped fresh parsley**

1. Brown sausage in skillet 6 to 8 minutes over medium-high heat, stirring to break up meat. Drain fat. Place sausage in 4½-quart **CROCK-POT®** slow cooker.

2. Stir in all remaining ingredients except parsley. Cover; cook on LOW 2 hours. Stir in parsley.

Makes 4 servings   *Prep Time:* 10 to 15 minutes   *Cook Time:* 2 hours (LOW)

Onion Marmalade

1 bottle (12 ounces) balsamic vinegar
1 bottle (12 ounces) white wine vinegar
3 tablespoons arrowroot or cornstarch
2 tablespoons water
1½ cups dark brown sugar
2 teaspoons cumin seeds
2 teaspoons coriander seeds
4 large yellow onions, halved and thinly sliced

1. With exhaust fan running, cook vinegars in large saucepan over high heat until reduced to ¼ cup. Sauce will be thick and syrupy. Remove from heat. Blend arrowroot and water in small cup. Add brown sugar, cumin, coriander and arrowroot mixture to sauce; blend well.

2. Place onions in 4½-quart **CROCK-POT®** slow cooker. Stir in vinegar mixture; mix well. Cover; cook on LOW 8 to 10 hours or HIGH 4 to 6 hours until onions are no longer crunchy. Stir occasionally to prevent sticking. Store in refrigerator for up to 2 weeks.

Tip: Serve as side dish or condiment with eggs, roasted vegetables and meats and on sandwiches.

Makes 5 cups	*Prep Time:* 40 minutes	*Cook Time:* 8 to 10 hours (LOW) or 4 to 6 hours (HIGH)

Blue Cheese Potatoes

2 pounds red potatoes, peeled and cut into ½-inch pieces
1¼ cups chopped green onions, divided
2 tablespoons olive oil, divided
1 teaspoon dried basil
½ teaspoon salt
¼ teaspoon black pepper
2 ounces crumbled blue cheese

1. Layer potatoes, 1 cup onions, 1 tablespoon oil, basil, salt and pepper in 4½-quart **CROCK-POT®** slow cooker. Cover; cook on LOW 7 hours or on HIGH 4 hours.

2. Gently stir in cheese and remaining 1 tablespoon oil. If **CROCK-POT®** slow cooker is on LOW turn to HIGH; cook an additional 5 minutes to allow flavors to blend. Transfer potatoes to serving platter and top with remaining ¼ cup onions.

Makes 5 servings	*Prep Time:* 15 minutes	*Cook Time:* 7 hours (LOW) or 4 hours (HIGH) plus 5 minutes (HIGH)

Simmered Red Beans with Rice

> **2** cans (about 15 ounces each) red beans, rinsed and drained
> **1** can (about 14 ounces) diced tomatoes, undrained
> **½** cup chopped celery
> **½** cup chopped green bell pepper
> **½** cup chopped green onions with tops
> **2** cloves garlic, minced
> **1** to 2 teaspoons hot pepper sauce
> **1** teaspoon Worcestershire sauce
> **1** bay leaf
> Hot cooked rice

1. Combine all ingredients except rice in 4½-quart **CROCK-POT®** slow cooker. Cover; cook on LOW 4 to 6 hours or on HIGH 2 to 3 hours.

2. Slightly mash mixture with potato masher to thicken. Continue to cook on LOW 30 to 60 minutes. Serve over rice.

Makes 6 (1-cup) servings   **Prep Time:** 15 minutes   **Cook Time:** 4 to 6 hours (LOW) or 2 to 3 hours (HIGH)

Polenta-Style Corn Casserole

- 1 **can (14½ ounces) chicken broth**
- ½ **cup cornmeal**
- 1 **can (7 ounces) corn, drained**
- 1 **can (4 ounces) diced green chilies, drained**
- ¼ **cup diced red bell pepper**
- ½ **teaspoon salt**
- ¼ **teaspoon black pepper**
- 1 **cup (4 ounces) shredded Cheddar cheese**

1. Pour broth into 4½-quart **CROCK-POT®** slow cooker. Whisk in cornmeal. Add corn, chilies, bell pepper, salt and pepper. Cover; cook on LOW 4 to 5 hours or on HIGH 2 to 3 hours.

2. Stir in cheese. Continue cooking, uncovered, 15 to 30 minutes or until cheese melts.

Serving Suggestion: Divide cooked corn mixture into lightly greased individual ramekins or spread in pie plate; cover and refrigerate. Serve at room temperature or warm in oven or microwave.

Makes 6 servings	Prep Time: 15 minutes	Cook Time: 4 to 5 hours (LOW) or 2 to 3 hours (HIGH)

Rustic Garlic Mashed Potatoes

    2 pounds baking potatoes, unpeeled and cut into ½-inch
        cubes
  ¼ cup water
    2 tablespoons butter, cut into ⅛-inch pieces
1¼ teaspoons salt
  ½ teaspoon garlic powder
  ¼ teaspoon black pepper
    1 cup milk

Place all ingredients except milk in 4½-quart **CROCK-POT®** slow cooker; toss to combine. Cover; cook on LOW 7 hours or on HIGH 4 hours. Add milk to potatoes. Mash potatoes with potato masher or electric mixer until smooth.

| **Makes 5 servings** | *Prep Time:* 10 to 15 minutes | *Cook Time:* 7 hours (LOW) or 4 hours (HIGH) |

Wild Rice and Mushroom Casserole

  2 tablespoons olive oil
  ½ medium red onion, finely diced
  1 large green pepper, finely diced
  8 ounces button mushrooms, thinly sliced
  2 cloves garlic, minced
  1 can (14 ounces) diced tomatoes, drained
  1 teaspoon dried oregano
  1 teaspoon paprika
  2 tablespoons butter
  2 tablespoons flour
1½ cups milk
  8 ounces shredded pepper jack, Cheddar or Swiss cheese
  1 teaspoon salt
  ½ teaspoon freshly ground black pepper
  2 cups wild rice, cooked according to package instructions

1. Heat oil in large skillet over medium heat. Add onion, green pepper and mushrooms. Sauté 5 to 6 minutes, stirring occasionally, or until vegetables soften. Add garlic, tomatoes, oregano and paprika. Continue to sauté until heated through. Remove to large mixing bowl to cool.

2. Melt butter in same skillet over medium heat; whisk in flour. Cook and stir until smooth and golden, about 4 to 5 minutes. Whisk in milk and bring to a boil. Whisk shredded cheese into boiling milk to produce rich, velvety sauce. Whisk in salt and pepper.

3. Combine cooked wild rice with sautéed vegetables in large mixing bowl. Fold in the cheese sauce and mix gently.

4. Coat the inside of the 4½-quart **CROCK-POT®** slow cooker with nonstick cooking spray. Pour in wild rice mixture. Cover and cook on LOW 4 to 6 hours or on HIGH 2 to 3 hours or until done.

Makes 4 to 6 servings **Prep Time:** 10 to 15 minutes **Cook Time:** 4 to 6 hours (LOW) or 2 to 3 hours (HIGH)

Traditional Sides 75

Orange-Spice Glazed Carrots

1 package (32 ounces) baby carrots
½ cup packed light brown sugar
½ cup orange juice
3 tablespoons butter or margarine
¾ teaspoon ground cinnamon
¼ teaspoon ground nutmeg
¼ cup cold water
2 tablespoons cornstarch

1. Combine all ingredients except water and cornstarch in 4½-quart **CROCK-POT®** slow cooker. Cover; cook on LOW 3½ to 4 hours or until carrots are crisp-tender.

2. Spoon carrots into serving bowl. Transfer juices to small saucepan; heat to a boil.

3. Mix water and cornstarch in cup or small bowl until smooth; stir into saucepan. Boil 1 minute or until thickened, stirring constantly. Spoon over carrots.

Makes 6 servings   *Prep Time:* 10 to 15 minutes   *Cook Time:* 3½ to 4 hours (LOW)

Macaroni and Cheese

6 **cups cooked macaroni**
2 **tablespoons butter**
4 **cups evaporated milk**
6 **cups Cheddar cheese, shredded**
2 **teaspoons salt**
½ **teaspoon black pepper**

In large mixing bowl, toss macaroni with butter. Stir in evaporated milk, cheese, salt and pepper; place in 4½-quart **CROCK-POT®** slow cooker. Cover; cook on HIGH 2 to 3 hours.

Tip: Make this mac 'n' cheese recipe more fun. Add some tasty mix-ins: diced green or red bell pepper, peas, hot dog slices, chopped tomato, browned ground beef or chopped onion. Be creative!

Makes 6 to 8 servings   *Prep Time:* 10 to 15 minutes   *Cook Time:* 2 to 3 hours (HIGH)

Wild Rice and Dried Cherry Risotto

1 cup dry-roasted salted peanuts
2 tablespoons sesame oil, divided
1 cup chopped onion
6 ounces uncooked wild rice
1 cup diced carrots
1 cup chopped green or red bell pepper
½ cup dried cherries
⅛ to ¼ teaspoon red pepper flakes
4 cups hot water
¼ cup teriyaki or soy sauce
1 teaspoon salt, or to taste

1. Coat 4½-quart **CROCK-POT®** slow cooker with nonstick cooking spray. Heat large skillet over medium-high heat until hot. Add peanuts. Cook and stir 2 to 3 minutes or until peanuts begin to brown. Transfer peanuts to plate; set aside.

2. Heat 2 teaspoons sesame oil in skillet until hot. Add onion. Cook and stir 6 minutes or until richly browned. Transfer to **CROCK-POT®** slow cooker.

3. Stir in wild rice, carrots, bell pepper, cherries, pepper flakes and water. Cover; cook on HIGH 3 hours.

4. Let stand 15 minutes, uncovered, until rice absorbs liquid. Stir in teriyaki sauce, peanuts, remaining oil and salt.

Makes 8 to 10 servings   *Prep Time:* 5 minutes   *Cook Time:* 3 hours (HIGH)

Roasted Summer Squash with Pine Nuts and Romano Cheese

2 tablespoons extra-virgin olive oil
½ cup chopped yellow onion
1 medium red bell pepper, cored, seeded and chopped
1 clove garlic, minced
3 medium zucchini, cut into ½-inch slices
3 medium summer squash, cut into ½-inch slices
½ cup chopped pine nuts
⅓ cup grated Romano cheese
1 teaspoon dried Italian seasoning
1 teaspoon salt
¼ teaspoon black pepper
1 tablespoon unsalted butter, cut into small cubes

1. Heat oil in skillet over medium-high heat until hot. Add onion, bell pepper and garlic. Cook and stir until onions are translucent and soft, about 10 minutes. Transfer to 4½-quart **CROCK-POT®** slow cooker.

2. Add zucchini and summer squash. Toss lightly.

3. Combine pine nuts, cheese, Italian seasoning, salt and pepper in small bowl. Fold half of cheese mixture into squash. Sprinkle remaining cheese mixture on top. Dot with butter. Cover; cook on LOW 4 to 6 hours.

Makes 6 to 8 servings　　　*Prep Time:* 15 to 20 minutes　　*Cook Time:* 4 to 6 hours (LOW)

Satisfying Soups and Stews

Old-Fashioned Split Pea Soup

    4 quarts chicken broth
    2 pounds dried split peas
    1 cup chopped ham
    ½ cup chopped onion
    ½ cup chopped celery
    2 teaspoons salt
    2 teaspoons black pepper

1. Place all ingredients in 6- or 7-quart **CROCK-POT®** slow cooker. Stir well to combine. Cover; cook on LOW 8 to 10 hours or on HIGH 4 to 6 hours or until peas are soft.

2. Mix with hand mixer or hand blender on LOW speed until smooth.

Makes 8 servings   *Prep Time:* 5 minutes   *Cook Time:* 8 to 10 hours (LOW) or
                                                                               4 to 6 hours (HIGH)

Braised Pork Shanks with Israeli Couscous and Root Vegetable Stew

4 pork shanks, bone in, skin removed (about 1½ pounds total)
   Coarse salt and black pepper, to taste
1 cup olive oil
4 large carrots, peeled and sliced diagonally into 1-inch segments, divided
4 stalks celery, sliced diagonally into 1-inch segments, divided
1 Spanish onion, peeled and quartered
4 cloves garlic, peeled and mashed
4 to 6 cups low-sodium chicken broth
2 cups dry white wine
¼ cup tomato paste
¼ cup white vinegar
2 tablespoons mustard oil* (optional)
1 tablespoon whole black peppercorns
   Israeli couscous, prepared according to package directions

*Mustard oil is available at Middle Eastern grocery stores or in the ethnic foods aisle of many large supermarkets.

1. Season shanks well with salt and pepper. Heat oil in large skillet over medium heat until hot. Brown shanks on all sides, turning as they brown. Transfer shanks and all but 2 tablespoons oil into 4½-quart **CROCK-POT®** slow cooker.

2. Add half of carrots, half of celery, onion and garlic to oil in skillet. Cook and stir over medium-low heat until vegetables are soft but not brown, about 5 minutes. Transfer to **CROCK-POT®** slow cooker.

3. Add broth, wine, tomato paste, vinegar, mustard oil, if desired, and peppercorns. Bring to a boil, stirring and scraping up any browned bits in

bottom of pan. Pour over shanks. Cover; cook on HIGH 2 hours, turning shanks every 20 minutes or so.

4. Remove shanks. Strain cooking liquid and discard solids. Return cooking liquid to **CROCK-POT®** slow cooker. Add remaining carrots and celery, and return shanks to **CROCK-POT®** slow cooker. Cover; cook on HIGH 1 hour.

5. Check shanks for doneness: Remove one and place it on a plate. Meat should be very soft but still attached to bone.

6. To serve, add cooked couscous to **CROCK-POT®** slow cooker to reheat, about 3 to 4 minutes. Using a slotted spoon place couscous, carrots and celery in shallow bowls. Place shank on top and spoon 2 to 3 ounces of cooking liquid into bowl.

Makes 4 servings	*Prep Time:* 30 minutes	*Cook Time:* 3 hours (HIGH)

Satisfying Soups and Stews 83

Italian Beef and Barley Soup

1 **boneless beef top sirloin steak (about 1½ pounds)**
1 **tablespoon vegetable oil**
4 **medium carrots or parsnips, cut into ¼-inch slices**
1 **cup chopped onion**
1 **teaspoon dried thyme**
½ **teaspoon dried rosemary**
¼ **teaspoon black pepper**
⅓ **cup uncooked pearl barley**
2 **cans (about 14 ounces each) beef broth**
1 **can (about 14 ounces) diced tomatoes with Italian seasoning, undrained**

1. Cut beef into 1-inch pieces. Heat oil over medium-high heat in large skillet. Brown beef on all sides; set aside.

2. Place carrots and onion in 4½-quart **CROCK-POT®** slow cooker; sprinkle with thyme, rosemary and pepper. Top with barley and beef. Pour broth and tomatoes over meat.

3. Cover; cook on LOW 8 to 10 hours or until beef is tender.

Tip: Choose pearl barley rather than quick-cooking barley because it will stand up to long cooking.

| Makes 6 servings | Prep Time: 20 minutes | Cook Time: 8 to 10 hours (LOW) |

Chicken Tortilla Soup

4 boneless, skinless chicken thighs

2 cans (15 ounces each) diced tomatoes, undrained

1 can (4 ounces) chopped mild green chiles, drained

½ to 1 cup chicken broth

1 yellow onion, diced

2 cloves garlic, minced

1 teaspoon ground cumin

Salt and black pepper, to taste

4 corn tortillas, sliced into ¼-inch strips

2 tablespoons chopped fresh cilantro

½ cup shredded Monterey Jack cheese

1 avocado, peeled, diced and tossed with lime juice to prevent browning

Lime wedges

1. Place chicken in 4½-quart **CROCK-POT®** slow cooker. Combine tomatoes with juice, chilies, ½ cup broth, onion, garlic and cumin in small bowl. Pour mixture over chicken.

2. Cover; cook on LOW 6 hours or on HIGH 3 hours or until chicken is tender. Remove chicken and shred with 2 forks. Return to cooking liquid. Adjust seasonings, adding salt and pepper and up to ½ cup more broth, if desired.

3. Just before serving, add tortillas and cilantro to **CROCK-POT®** slow cooker. Stir to blend. Serve in soup bowls, topping each serving with cheese, avocado and a squeeze of lime juice.

Makes 4 to 6 servings   *Prep Time:* 10 minutes   *Cook Time:* 6 hours (LOW) or 3 hours (HIGH)

Niku Jaga (Japanese Beef Stew)

2 tablespoons vegetable oil
2 pounds beef stew meat, cut into 1-inch cubes
4 medium carrots, peeled and diagonally sliced
3 medium Yukon Gold potatoes, peeled and chopped
1 white onion, peeled and chopped
1 cup water
½ cup Japanese sake or dry white wine
¼ cup sugar
¼ cup soy sauce
1 teaspoon salt

1. Heat oil in skillet over medium heat until hot. Sear beef on all sides, turning as it browns. Transfer beef to 4½-quart **CROCK-POT®** slow cooker.

2. Add remaining ingredients. Stir well to combine. Cover; cook on LOW 10 to 12 hours or on HIGH 4 to 6 hours.

Makes 6 to 8 servings   *Prep Time:* 10 minutes   *Cook Time:* 10 to 12 hours (LOW) or 4 to 6 hours (HIGH)

Mediterranean Tomato, Oregano and Orzo Soup

2 tablespoons extra-virgin olive oil

1 large yellow onion, cut into wedges

3½ cups fresh tomatoes, peeled* and hand-crushed

2 cups butternut squash, peeled and cut into ½-inch cubes

1 cup carrots, peeled and cut into matchstick pieces

½ cup zucchini, cleaned and sliced

1 tablespoon minced fresh bay leaves or 3 whole dried bay leaves

1 tablespoon chopped fresh oregano

1 can (15 ounces) garbanzo beans, rinsed and drained

2 cups chicken broth

1 clove garlic, minced

1 teaspoon ground cumin

¾ teaspoon ground allspice

½ teaspoon salt

¼ teaspoon black pepper

1½ cups dried orzo pasta

To peel tomatoes, place 1 at a time in simmering water for about 10 seconds. (Add 30 seconds if tomatoes are not fully ripened.) Immediately plunge into a bowl of cold water for another 10 seconds. Peel skin with a knife.

1. Heat oil in skillet over medium heat until hot. Add onion. Cook and stir until translucent and soft, about 10 minutes.

2. Add tomatoes, squash, carrots, zucchini, bay leaves and oregano to skillet. Cook and stir 25 to 30 minutes longer. Transfer to 4½-quart **CROCK-POT®** slow cooker.

3. Add remaining ingredients, except orzo pasta. Cover; cook on LOW 7 to 8 hours or on HIGH 4 to 5 hours.

4. Increase temperature to HIGH. Add orzo. Cover; cook 30 to 45 minutes or until pasta is done. (Remove dried bay leaves before serving, if used.)

Makes 6 servings   *Prep Time:* 45 minutes   *Cook Time:* 7 to 8 hours (LOW) or 4 to 5 hours (HIGH), plus 30 to 345 minutes (HIGH)

Satisfying Soups and Stews   91

Chicken and Sweet Potato Stew

4 boneless, skinless chicken breasts, cut into bite-size pieces
2 medium sweet potatoes, peeled and cubed
2 medium Yukon Gold potatoes, peeled and cubed
2 medium carrots, peeled and cut into ½-inch slices
1 can (28 ounces) whole stewed tomatoes
1 teaspoon salt
1 teaspoon paprika
1 teaspoon celery seeds
½ teaspoon freshly ground black pepper
⅛ teaspoon ground cinnamon
⅛ teaspoon ground nutmeg
1 cup fat-free, low-sodium chicken broth
¼ cup fresh basil, chopped

1. Combine chicken, potatoes, carrots, tomatoes, salt, paprika, celery seeds, pepper, cinnamon, nutmeg and broth in 4½-quart **CROCK-POT®** slow cooker.

2. Cover; cook on LOW 6 to 8 hours or on HIGH 3 to 4 hours.

3. Sprinkle with basil just before serving.

Note: This light stew has an Indian influence and offers excellent flavor without the fat.

Tip: You may double all the ingredients and prepare in a 7-quart **CROCK-POT®** slow cooker.

Makes 6 servings   *Prep Time:* 15 minutes   *Cook Time:* 6 to 8 hours (LOW) 3 to 4 hours (HIGH)

Caramelized French Onion Soup

4 **extra-large sweet onions, peeled**
4 **tablespoons (½ stick) butter**
2 **cups dry white wine**
8 **cups beef or vegetable broth, divided**
2 **cups water**
1 **tablespoon minced fresh thyme**
6 **cups large seasoned croutons**
1 **cup Swiss or Gruyère cheese, shredded**

1. Cut each onion into quarters. Cut each quarter into ¼-inch-thick slices. Heat skillet over medium heat until hot. Add butter and onions. Cook, stirring every 7 to 8 minutes. Transfer to 4½-quart **CROCK-POT®** slow cooker when onions are soft and caramelized, about 45 to 50 minutes total.

2. Add wine to skillet and let liquid reduce to about ½ cup, simmering about 15 minutes. Transfer to **CROCK-POT®** slow cooker.

3. Add broth, water and thyme to **CROCK-POT®** slow cooker. Cover; cook on HIGH 2½ hours or until thoroughly heated.

4. To serve, ladle soup into individual ovenproof soup bowls. Place 1 crouton on top, and sprinkle cheese over crouton. Preheat oven broiler and place bowls on top shelf of oven. Broil 3 to 5 minutes or until cheese is melted and golden. Serve immediately.

Makes 6 servings   *Prep Time:* About 1 hour   *Cook Time:* 2½ hours (HIGH)

Grandma Ruth's Minestrone

1 **pound ground beef**
1 **cup dried red beans**
1 **package (16 ounces) frozen mixed vegetables**
2 **cans (8 ounces each) tomato sauce**
1 **can (14 ounces) diced tomatoes, drained**
¼ **head shredded cabbage**
1 **cup chopped onions**
1 **cup chopped celery**
½ **cup chopped fresh parsley**
1 **tablespoon dried basil**
1 **tablespoon Italian seasoning**
1 **teaspoon salt**
1 **teaspoon black pepper**
1 **cup cooked macaroni**

1. Combine ground beef and beans in 4½-quart **CROCK-POT®** slow cooker. Cover; cook on HIGH 2 hours.

2. Add all remaining ingredients except macaroni and stir to blend. Cover; cook on LOW 6 to 8 hours or until beans are tender.

3. Stir in macaroni. Cover; cook HIGH for 1 hour.

Makes 4 servings	*Prep Time:* 15 minutes	*Cook Time:* 3 hours (HIGH) plus 6 to 8 hours (LOW)

Wild Mushroom Beef Stew

1½ **to 2 pounds beef stew meat, cut into 1-inch cubes**
2 **tablespoons all-purpose flour**
½ **teaspoon salt**
½ **teaspoon black pepper**
1½ **cups beef broth**
1 **teaspoon Worcestershire sauce**
1 **clove garlic, minced**
1 **bay leaf**
1 **teaspoon paprika**
4 **shiitake mushrooms, sliced**
2 **medium carrots, sliced**
2 **medium potatoes, diced**
1 **small white onion, chopped**
1 **rib celery, sliced**

1. Put beef into 4½-quart **CROCK-POT®** slow cooker. Mix together flour, salt and pepper and sprinkle over meat; stir to coat each piece of meat with flour. Add the remaining ingredients and stir to mix well.

2. Cover; cook on LOW 10 to 12 hours or on HIGH 4 to 6 hours. Stir the stew before serving.

Note: This classic beef stew is given a twist with the addition of flavorful shiitake mushrooms. If fresh shiitake mushrooms are unavailable in your local grocery store, you can substitute other mushrooms of your choice. For extra punch, add a few dried porcini mushrooms to the stew.

Makes 5 servings	**Prep Time:** 15 to 20 minutes	**Cook Time:** 10 to 12 hours (LOW) or 4 to 6 hours (HIGH)

Chicken Fiesta Soup

4 boneless, skinless chicken breasts, cooked and shredded
1 can (14½ ounces) stewed tomatoes, drained
2 cans (4 ounces each) chopped green chiles
1 can (28 ounces) enchilada sauce
1 can (14½ ounces) chicken broth
1 cup finely chopped onions
2 cloves garlic, minced
1 teaspoon ground cumin
1 teaspoon chili powder
¾ teaspoon pepper
1 teaspoon salt
¼ cup finely chopped fresh cilantro
1 cup frozen whole kernel corn
1 yellow squash, diced
1 zucchini, diced
8 tostada shells, crumbled
8 ounces shredded Cheddar cheese

1. Combine chicken, tomatoes, chiles, enchilada sauce, broth, onions, garlic, cumin, chili powder, pepper, salt, cilantro, corn, squash and zucchini in 4½-quart **CROCK-POT®** slow cooker.

2. Cover; cook on LOW 8 hours. To serve, fill individual bowls with soup. Garnish with crumbled tostada shells and cheese.

| Makes 8 servings | *Prep Time:* 5 minutes | *Cook Time:* 8 hours (LOW) |

Creamy Crab Bisque

4 **cups heavy cream**
3 **cups fresh crab meat, flaked and picked**
3 **tablespoons unsalted butter**
2 **teaspoons grated lemon peel**
1 **teaspoon lemon juice**
½ **teaspoon ground nutmeg**
¼ **teaspoon ground allspice**
3 **tablespoons dry red wine**
½ **cup prepared mandlen,* ground into crumbs**

Mandlen, sometimes called "soup nuts," are small nugget-like crackers made from matzo meal. They're available in the ethnic foods aisle of many supermarkets. Round, rich butter crackers may be substituted.

1. Combine cream, crab, butter, lemon peel, lemon juice, nutmeg and allspice in 4½-quart **CROCK-POT®** slow cooker. Stir well to combine. Cover; cook on LOW 1 to 2 hours.

2. To serve, stir in wine. Add mandlen crumbs to thicken soup and stir again. Continue cooking 10 minutes longer.

Makes 6 to 8 servings | **Prep Time:** 5 minutes | **Cook Time:** 1 to 2 hours (LOW)

Roasted Corn and Red Pepper Chowder

    2 tablespoons extra-virgin olive oil
    2 cups fresh corn kernels or frozen corn, thawed
    1 red bell pepper, cored, seeded and diced
    2 green onions, sliced
    4 cups chicken broth
    2 baking potatoes, peeled and diced
    1 teaspoon salt
    ½ teaspoon black pepper
    1 can (13 ounces) evaporated milk
    2 tablespoons minced flat-leaf parsley

1. Heat oil in skillet over medium heat until hot. Add corn, bell pepper and onions. Cook and stir until vegetables are tender and lightly browned, about 7 to 8 minutes. Transfer to 4½-quart **CROCK-POT®** slow cooker.

2. Add broth, potatoes, salt and pepper. Stir well to combine. Cover; cook on LOW 7 to 9 hours or on HIGH 4 to 5 hours.

3. Thirty minutes before serving, add milk. Stir well to combine and continue cooking. To serve, garnish with parsley.

Makes 4 servings	*Prep Time:* 15 minutes	*Cook Time:* 7 to 9 hours (LOW) or 4 to 5 hours (HIGH)

Timeless Treats

Spicy Apple Butter

> **5** pounds tart cooking apples (McIntosh, Granny Smith, Rome Beauty or York Imperial), peeled, cored and quartered (about 10 large apples)
>
> **1** cup sugar
>
> **½** cup apple juice
>
> **2** teaspoons ground cinnamon
>
> **½** teaspoon ground cloves
>
> **½** teaspoon ground allspice

1. Combine all ingredients in 4½-quart **CROCK-POT®** slow cooker. Cover; cook on LOW 8 to 10 hours or until apples are very tender.

2. Mash apples with potato masher. Cook, uncovered, on LOW 2 hours or until thickened, stirring occasionally to prevent sticking.

Serving Suggestion: Homemade apple butter is a great alternative to store-bought jam or jelly on your favorite toast or muffin. For an instant dessert, try toasting a few slices of pound cake and spreading apple butter on them!

| Makes about 6 cups | **Prep Time:** 25 minutes | **Cook Time:** 10 to 12 hours |

Christmas Plum Pudding

2½ cups milk

4 eggs, slightly beaten

10 slices white bread, cut into 2-inch cubes

2¼ cups all-purpose flour

2¼ cups packed light brown sugar

5 teaspoons ground cinnamon

2 teaspoons baking soda

2 teaspoons ground cloves

2 teaspoons ground mace

1 teaspoon salt

½ cup orange juice

3 teaspoons vanilla

3 cups raisins

2 cups dried plums

1 cup dried candied fruit mix

1. Coat inside of 4½-quart **CROCK-POT®** slow cooker with nonstick cooking spray. Combine milk and eggs in large bowl. Add bread; set aside to soak.

2. Combine flour, brown sugar, cinnamon, baking soda, cloves, mace and salt. Mix in orange juice and vanilla, stirring until smooth. Add raisins, plums and candied fruit.

3. Place bread in **CROCK-POT®** slow cooker. Pour fruit mixture over bread. Cover; cook on LOW 6 to 7 hours or on HIGH 2 to 4 hours. Serve warm.

| Makes 8 to 10 servings | *Prep Time:* 15 minutes | *Cook Time:* 6 to 7 hours (LOW) or 2 to 4 hours (HIGH) |

Steamed Southern Sweet Potato Custard

1 **can (16 ounces) cut sweet potatoes, drained**
1 **can (12 ounces) evaporated milk, divided**
½ **cup packed light brown sugar**
2 **eggs, lightly beaten**
1 **teaspoon ground cinnamon**
½ **teaspoon ground ginger**
¼ **teaspoon salt**
   Whipped cream
   Ground nutmeg

1. Process sweet potatoes with ¼ cup evaporated milk in food processor or blender until smooth. Add remaining milk, brown sugar, eggs, cinnamon, ginger and salt; process until well blended. Pour into ungreased 1-quart soufflé dish. Cover tightly with foil. Crumple large sheet (about 15×12 inches) of foil; place in bottom of 4½-quart **CROCK-POT®** slow cooker. Pour 2 cups water over foil. Make foil handles.*

2. Transfer dish to 4½-quart **CROCK-POT®** slow cooker using foil handles. Cover; cook on HIGH 2½ to 3 hours or until skewer inserted into center comes out clean.

3. Use foil strips to lift dish; transfer to wire rack. Uncover; let stand 30 minutes. Garnish with whipped cream and nutmeg.

Makes 4 servings   *Prep Time:* 15 minutes   *Cook Time:* 2½ to 3 hours (HIGH)

*To make foil handles, tear off 3 (18×3-inch) strips of heavy-duty foil. Crisscross the strips so they resemble the spokes of a wheel. Place the dish or food in the center of the strips. Pull the foil strips up and over the dish and place it into the slow cooker. Leave the foil strips in while the food cooks, so you can easily lift the item out again when it is finished cooking.

Mexican Chocolate Bread Pudding

1½ **cups light cream**

4 **ounces unsweetened chocolate, coarsely chopped**

2 **eggs, beaten**

½ **cup sugar**

¾ **teaspoon ground cinnamon**

½ **teaspoon ground allspice**

1 **teaspoon vanilla**

⅛ **teaspoon salt**

½ **cup currants**

3 **cups Hawaiian-style sweet bread, challah or rich egg bread, cut into ½-inch cubes**

Whipped cream (optional)

Chopped macadamia nuts (optional)

1. Heat cream in large saucepan. Add chocolate and stir until chocolate melts.

2. Combine eggs, sugar, cinnamon, allspice, vanilla and salt in medium bowl. Stir in currants. Add to chocolate mixture. Stir well to combine. Pour into 4½-quart **CROCK-POT®** slow cooker.

3. Gently fold in bread cubes using plastic spatula. Cover; cook on HIGH 3 to 4 hours or until knife inserted near center comes out clean.

4. Serve warm or chilled. If desired, top with generous dollop of whipped cream and sprinkling of nuts.

Makes 6 to 8 servings   *Prep Time:* 15 minutes   *Cook Time:* 3 to 4 hours (HIGH)

Pumpkin Bread Pudding

Bread Pudding

- 2 cups whole milk
- 2 tablespoons butter
- 3 large eggs
- 1 cup puréed pumpkin
- 2 teaspoons vanilla
- ½ cup packed dark brown sugar
- 1 tablespoon ground cinnamon
- ½ teaspoon ground nutmeg
- ¼ teaspoon salt
- 16 slices cinnamon raisin bread, torn into small pieces (8 cups total)

Sauce

- ½ cup (1 stick) butter
- ½ cup packed dark brown sugar
- ½ cup heavy cream
- 2 tablespoons bourbon (optional)

1. Lightly coat inside of 3½- to 4-quart **CROCK-POT®** slow cooker with nonstick cooking spray.

2. To make pudding, place milk and butter in microwavable bowl; heat in microwave on HIGH 2½ to 3 minutes or until very hot.

3. Combine eggs, pumpkin, vanilla, sugar, cinnamon, nutmeg and salt in large bowl. Whisk until well blended. Add hot milk; stir until well blended. Add bread cubes; toss gently to coat completely.

4. Place bread mixture in **CROCK-POT®** slow cooker; cover. Cook on HIGH 2 hours or until knife inserted into center comes out clean. Turn off heat. Uncover; let stand 15 minutes.

5. To make sauce, stir butter, sugar and cream in small saucepan. Bring to a boil over high heat, stirring frequently. Remove from heat. Stir in bourbon, if desired. Spoon bread pudding into individual bowls and top with sauce.

Note: Sauce should be used immediately.

Makes 8 servings	*Prep Time:* 15 minutes	*Cook Time:* 2 hours (HIGH)

Rum and Cherry Cola Fudge Spoon Cake

Cake

½ cup cola
½ cup dried sour cherries
1 cup chocolate milk
½ cup (1 stick) unsalted butter, melted
2 teaspoons vanilla
1½ cups all-purpose flour
½ cup ground sweet chocolate
½ cup granulated sugar
2½ teaspoons baking powder
½ teaspoon salt

Topping

1¼ cups vanilla cola
¼ cup dark rum
½ cup ground sweet chocolate
½ cup granulated sugar
½ cup packed brown sugar

1. Coat 4½-quart **CROCK-POT®** slow cooker with nonstick cooking spray. Bring cola and dried cherries to a boil in saucepan. Remove from heat; let cherries stand 30 minutes.

2. Combine chocolate milk, melted butter and vanilla in small bowl. Combine flour, ground chocolate, granulated sugar, baking powder and salt in medium bowl; stir to mix well. Make a well in center of dry ingredients; add milk mixture and stir until smooth. Stir cherry mixture into batter. Pour into **CROCK-POT®** slow cooker.

3. To prepare topping, bring vanilla cola and rum to a boil in saucepan. Remove from heat. Add ground chocolate and sugars; stir until smooth. Gently pour over batter. Do not stir. Cover; cook on HIGH 2½ hours or until cake is puffed and top layer has set.

4. Turn off heat. Let stand, covered, 30 minutes. Serve warm. Garnish as desired.

Makes 8 to 10 servings   *Prep Time:* 15 minutes   *Cook Time:* 2½ hours (HIGH)

Brownie Bottoms

½ cup brown sugar
¾ cup water
2 tablespoons unsweetened cocoa powder
2½ cups packaged brownie mix
1 package (2¾ ounces) instant chocolate pudding mix
½ cup milk chocolate chip morsels
2 eggs, beaten
3 tablespoons butter or margarine, melted

1. Coat 4½-quart **CROCK-POT®** slow cooker with nonstick cooking spray. In small saucepan, combine brown sugar, water and cocoa powder; bring to a boil.

2. Combine brownie mix, pudding mix, morsels, eggs and butter in medium bowl; stir until well blended. Spread batter into prepared **CROCK-POT®** slow cooker; pour boiling sugar mixture over batter. Cover; cook on HIGH for 1½ hours.

3. Turn off heat and let stand, covered, 30 minutes. Serve warm.

Note: Serve this warm chocolate dessert with whipped cream or ice cream.

Tip: To make a double batch use a 5-, 6- or 7-quart **CROCK-POT®** slow cooker and double all ingredients.

Makes 6 servings	Prep Time: 15 minutes	Cook Time: 1½ hours

Strawberry Rhubarb Crisp

Fruit

> 4 **cups sliced hulled strawberries**
>
> 4 **cups diced rhubarb (about 5 stalks), cut into ½-inch dice**
>
> 1½ **cups granulated sugar**
>
> 2 **tablespoons lemon juice**
>
> 1½ **tablespoons cornstarch, plus water (optional)**

Topping

> 1 **cup all-purpose flour**
>
> 1 **cup old-fashioned oats**
>
> ½ **cup granulated sugar**
>
> ½ **cup brown sugar**
>
> ½ **teaspoon ground ginger**
>
> ½ **teaspoon ground nutmeg**
>
> ½ **cup butter (1 stick), cut into pieces**
>
> ½ **cup sliced almonds, toasted***

*To toast almonds, spread in single layer on baking sheet. Bake in preheated 350°F oven 8 to 10 minutes or until golden brown, stirring frequently.

1. Prepare fruit. Coat 4½-quart **CROCK-POT®** slow cooker with nonstick cooking spray. Place strawberries, rhubarb, granulated sugar and lemon juice in **CROCK-POT®** slow cooker and mix well. Cook on HIGH 1½ hours or until fruit is tender.

2. If fruit is dry after cooking, add a little water. If fruit has too much liquid, mix cornstarch with a small amount of water and stir into fruit. Cook on HIGH an additional 15 minutes or until cooking liquid is thickened.

3. Preheat oven to 375°F. Prepare topping. Combine flour, oats, sugars, ginger and nutmeg in medium bowl. Cut in butter using pastry blender or 2 knives until mixture resembles coarse crumbs. Stir in almonds.

4. Remove lid from **CROCK-POT**® slow cooker and gently sprinkle topping onto fruit. Transfer stoneware to oven. Bake 15 to 20 minutes or until topping begins to brown.

Makes 8 servings   *Prep Time:* 20 minutes   *Cook Time:* 1½ to 1¾ hours (HIGH)

Timeless Treats   119

Hot Fudge Cake

1¾ cups packed light brown sugar, divided
2 cups all-purpose flour
¼ cup plus 3 tablespoons unsweetened cocoa powder,
    divided, plus additional for dusting (optional)
2 teaspoons baking powder
1 teaspoon salt
1 cup milk
4 tablespoons (½ stick) butter, melted
1 teaspoon vanilla
3½ cups boiling water

1. Coat 4½-quart **CROCK-POT®** slow cooker with nonstick cooking spray or butter. Mix 1 cup sugar, flour, 3 tablespoons cocoa powder, baking powder and salt in medium bowl. Stir in milk, butter and vanilla. Mix until well blended. Pour into **CROCK-POT®** slow cooker.

2. Blend remaining ¾ cup sugar and ¼ cup cocoa powder in small bowl. Sprinkle evenly over cake batter. Pour in boiling water. Do not stir.

3. Cover; cook on HIGH 1¼ to 1½ hours or until toothpick inserted into center comes out clean. Allow cake to rest 10 minutes; invert onto serving platter or scoop into serving dishes. Serve warm; dust with cocoa powder, if desired.

Makes 6 to 8 servings   *Prep Time:* 15 minutes   *Cook Time:* 1¼ to 1½ hours (HIGH)

METRIC CONVERSION CHART

VOLUME MEASUREMENTS (dry)

1/8 teaspoon = 0.5 mL
1/4 teaspoon = 1 mL
1/2 teaspoon = 2 mL
3/4 teaspoon = 4 mL
1 teaspoon = 5 mL
1 tablespoon = 15 mL
2 tablespoons = 30 mL
1/4 cup = 60 mL
1/3 cup = 75 mL
1/2 cup = 125 mL
2/3 cup = 150 mL
3/4 cup = 175 mL
1 cup = 250 mL
2 cups = 1 pint = 500 mL
3 cups = 750 mL
4 cups = 1 quart = 1 L

VOLUME MEASUREMENTS (fluid)

1 fluid ounce (2 tablespoons) = 30 mL
4 fluid ounces (1/2 cup) = 125 mL
8 fluid ounces (1 cup) = 250 mL
12 fluid ounces (1 1/2 cups) = 375 mL
16 fluid ounces (2 cups) = 500 mL

WEIGHTS (mass)

1/2 ounce = 15 g
1 ounce = 30 g
3 ounces = 90 g
4 ounces = 120 g
8 ounces = 225 g
10 ounces = 285 g
12 ounces = 360 g
16 ounces = 1 pound = 450 g

DIMENSIONS

1/16 inch = 2 mm
1/8 inch = 3 mm
1/4 inch = 6 mm
1/2 inch = 1.5 cm
3/4 inch = 2 cm
1 inch = 2.5 cm

OVEN TEMPERATURES

250°F = 120°C
275°F = 140°C
300°F = 150°C
325°F = 160°C
350°F = 180°C
375°F = 190°C
400°F = 200°C
425°F = 220°C
450°F = 230°C

BAKING PAN SIZES

Utensil	Size in Inches/Quarts	Metric Volume	Size in Centimeters
Baking or Cake Pan (square or rectangular)	8×8×2	2 L	20×20×5
	9×9×2	2.5 L	23×23×5
	12×8×2	3 L	30×20×5
	13×9×2	3.5 L	33×23×5
Loaf Pan	8×4×3	1.5 L	20×10×7
	9×5×3	2 L	23×13×7
Round Layer Cake Pan	8×1½	1.2 L	20×4
	9×1½	1.5 L	23×4
Pie Plate	8×1¼	750 mL	20×3
	9×1¼	1 L	23×3
Baking Dish or Casserole	1 quart	1 L	—
	1½ quarts	1.5 L	—
	2 quarts	2 L	—